AF110226

Anoushka Sawant

BLUEROSE PUBLISHERS
India | U.K.

Copyright © Anoushka Sawant 2024

All rights reserved by author. No part of this publication may be reproduced, stored in a retrieval system or transmitted in any form or by any means, electronic, mechanical, photocopying, recording or otherwise, without the prior permission of the author. Although every precaution has been taken to verify the accuracy of the information contained herein, the publisher assumes no responsibility for any errors or omissions. No liability is assumed for damages that may result from the use of information contained within.

BlueRose Publishers takes no responsibility for any damages, losses, or liabilities that may arise from the use or misuse of the information, products, or services provided in this publication.

For permissions requests or inquiries regarding this publication,
please contact:

BLUEROSE PUBLISHERS
www.BlueRoseONE.com
info@bluerosepublishers.com
+91 8882 898 898
+4407342408967

ISBN: 978-93-6783-324-7

Cover Design: Sadhna Kumari
Typesetting: Pooja Sharma

First Edition: November 2024

PREFACE

Poetry to me, began as a means of creative illustration. Over time, however, it turned into a medium of escape. In a world controlled by everyone but me, writing, expressing, and interpreting reality the way I viewed it, instilled a sense of conviction and freedom. As you skim through the poems, you may recognize the change in my style of writing from the previous book that I published as a late teenager. This collection views the world with depth and empathy, there is place for mistakes, anger, acceptance and learning to love the little things about life. A young me, wrote in confinement; she wanted to be unbiased and meticulous. Unlike that, this medley is like the roar of a young woman learning to use the intricate moments of life to understand the concept of happiness, sometimes embrace it, and other times question it. You will find a spectrum of mosaics to relate to- friendship, success, ambition, and creativity, to name a few. I hope this book feels like a soft hug to everyone who feels emotions so deeply but cannot always find the words to express themselves, which is why I call it *'**The Oeuvre**'* – The complete collection of an author's work.

ACKNOWLEDGMENTS

My deepest gratitude to my loving parents, **Mrs. Smita Sawant** and **Dr. Raj Sawant**, I appreciate the grace in life because they showed it to me. I would also like to thank my brother **Aryaman,** who beyond the capacity of words, stood by me. And lastly, my closest clan- **Vinayak Tandon, Jay Mehta and Heth Shah**; every moment of strength, success and applause, I owe to these three close friends who make me believe in the beauty of life. And of course, I owe it to all well-wishers and engaging audiences who encouraged me on social media platforms. Lastly, I'd like to thank **Blue Rose Publications** for providing me with such a great opportunity.

CONTENTS

1. A SLICE OF PARADISE 1
2. CASTLES BY THE BAY 5
3. COLOURS 9
4. CIRCLE 11
5. DEAR STRANGER 15
6. DIFFERENT 19
7. DO YOU FEEL THAT WAY AS WELL? 23
8. ERASING 27
9. ERASING II 31
10. ESCAPE 35
11. EYES 39
12. FOR THE LOVE OF IT 43
13. FRAGILE 47
14. HE CAN NEVER 51
15. I AM NOT A WRITER 55
16. I BELONG 59
17. I KNOW 63
18. IMBALANCE 67
19. LOVED ME LONG BEFORE 69
20. MOTHER 71
21. MOTHER, OH MOTHER MINE 75
22. ONCE AGAIN 79
23. OUR CHANCE 83
24. PARADOX 87

25. SHINE 91

26. SPIELS 93

27. THERE RESIDES THIS HEAVINESS 97

28. THE CITY 101

29. THE MIND 103

30. THE PRICE 107

31. THEY ASK ME 111

32. THIS IS HER 115

33. UNTIL 119

34. WALK 121

35. WALLS 125

36. WAS IT WORTH? 129

37. WHAT AM I HERE FOR? 133

38. WHO WILL TEACH ME? 137

39. WHY? 141

40. YEARS I THINK IT TOOK ME 145

41. YOU AND I 149

42. ZILLION OLD 153

1. A SLICE OF PARADISE

A roof of stars
a blanket of grass
a cup of hailstones
an eternity of unknowns,
Of emeralds a jar
ocean of sunflowers
berries that sway
like blood in my veins,
A crumpled dream
a star-crossed longing
a box of aroma
of candles cigars,
A den of butterflies
a robe of silk
an iris coloured
as are sea beds galaxies,
Some garlands of ice
some frantic caramel pies
some infinity to wrap
on despair's thighs,
A tingle of poetry
a drop of pain
some stories to carry

from dawn to grave,
A bowl of honey
wrinkled old shelves alimony,
staring into
your big brown-tinged eyes
a trench of calm this is
they probably disguise, call it
a slice of paradise.

2. CASTLES BY THE BAY

You will all grow up
and forget these castles by the bay
swinging back and forth
in the wooden chair
my mother would say,
These poems will be forgotten
your sketchbooks will rust
last time today
this football will show up on turf,
9-5 will gallop in deadlines
Pâtissiers will forward emails
all singers will miss trains
enthusiasm down the drain,
One day will be the last
and you won't even know when
money and race will chase
long before your dreams catch breath,
One day you will all grow up
go offline your virtual games
one day you will log out
the last very strike of flames,

Doe eyes of hope will open
to the reality of shame
a lifeless world
of glass skyscrapers
all alike
all dressed the same,
Your photographs will dry
years will pass by
your colours from childhood
will wash away
and once again you will live to tell
your children how
you forgot castles by the bay.

3. COLOURS

Blue
is the oceans- monstrous, waves unremitting
the sky of cotton balls, an arena of fluffy candy,
Green
is the tropical, home to nestlings'
divine mother of all, flowers to saplings,
Yellow
is the reflection, of rays on windows
and windows on mirrors,
sand and plush fields, staring at each other.,
Red
is the fruits, berries and cherries and apples
and the fragrance, a bush of lilies
and poppies and roses,
White
is the spinning of all these shades
cheek by cheek, hands intertwined
a tapestry of beautiful creations
on most days nature tranquilizes.

4. CIRCLE

It is a circle with no bounds
that begins as an infant pleased
showering play of hide and seek
an innocent soul cannot yet walk
merely recognizing voices, gasping to talk,
And then slightly you begin to evolve
warm hugs of non-judgmental friendship
some sheepish nights of teenage boy bands
butterflies of forevers
some lessons of betrayal,
Phases of the moon with perpetual utility
tossed like balls of work and salary
and when both hands juggle well
bring in a bride, settle in children!
Then inherent a pinnacle you reach
unbothered uninterested unhinged
by some thoughts that yesterday were a pinch
for now all you want,
is for your little universe to blossom safe and sound,
Some more seasons brush by,
when close ones diverge so you approach old smiles,
take a pause, decide to carry on
for all those wishes that were once selfishly just yours,

Take pictures more often and you relive every sip
learn more about letting go, basics of being kind
watch flowers grow, blood drift away, flow,
and youth effortlessly blossom into old,
Only to once again return to a child-
an innocent infant that can no longer walk
merely recognizing voices, gasping to talk,
losing teeth and watching hair fall,
That is what to believe the novelty of life is
of being a mortal with less than limited time
to feel thrill and lows, success and blows
to value moments, time the clock
for you never know when
the second hand is about to stop.

5. DEAR STRANGER

Dear stranger
that I'd take a bullet for
may you scale every cliff
that meets your eye
may twenty one gears catalyse your ascend
to every new cycle, of adventures that lie
may your life be a storybook
of all the tunes you hum
and all the lives you adorn
all your laughter captured
in places you've always loved,
Dear stranger
that I'd take a bullet for
may you heal from things
that are still hard to speak about
may you hear and know and speak
all about those theories you read aloud
may every morning build new doors
may every night return you home
a train of celebration may this life be
baskets of joy, garlands of applause,
Dear stranger
that I'd take a bullet for

may your eyes never stop widening
as you prattle about your beliefs likes
may you find meaning in
all the things hard to describe
may you spring and bounce and hop and leap
in the lap of every day, let alone reside thrill,
Dear stranger
that I'd take a bullet for
may you be blessed
with all the freedom in this life
may your scars be, the ticket to triumph
and if one day you hear the moon
calling you by your name
don't be surprised for
I tell her about this stranger
every single day.

6. DIFFERENT

How much skill it must've taken
to craft bodies each unique
sit differently, that sip differently
talk about the same things
with divergent thesis
that think at variance
comprehend like chalk and cheese,
Accents unalike temperaments too
tastes that change as winds do
every person unlike you
in an attempt to confess their pride
will teach you something about yourself
and whether you choose to clash or care
be assured of love affairs that begin
when you learn from assorted despairs,
Mother would say
'we look not for perfections but scars in people'
because loss, doom, inhibitions
unite walks of all lives
rubbernecking for emotions, effortlessness
of who to be like
who to not
what to select, leave untouched

and somewhere in the chase I count on
empathy to draw a line,
I marvel at us, rebels and saints
extreme and abstemious hues
ability to slit throats, ability to comfort
separated by waters, distant by beliefs
you and I are blurred
yet, simultaneously
you and I are limpid.

7. DO YOU FEEL THAT WAY AS WELL?

Do you feel that way as well?
that length you are ready to go
just to understand them,
that anticipation you place
as you rest yourself in their shoes
how habitually you push
everything aside for them
but they catch up with you
only when free time decides you fit in,
how intricately you carve
every surface that will,
make them laugh so hard,
you too 'okay' things
even when they're not?
you give a lot ahead that for what
you can perhaps account?
you feel this longing in your heart
wondering if anyone there is
equipped to live up to the mark?

Wishing off-guard someone caught
insisted on sitting with you long enough
even after you've declared you're fine?
do you feel that way as well?
the more you learn about people
the more you love your pet,
to declare there is none to lose
what a sharp knife there is,
daggered into your chest?
the more chances you place
the more disappointments you see ways
and still in every heart beat you bite your tongue
because that was taught as a way
of protecting people?
Do you feel that way as well?
that bare minimum is such a task
when you offer top tier at every single glance?
that every new hope is just
about another lousy losing game
every time you offer a piece of yourself
you are just about losing again.

8. ERASING

You should have seen him
when he spoke about his dreams
his love for the mountains
sparkling in his eyes
hunger for continents enormous
sliding in his delirious tone
when he swayed his fingers
to paint into words oceans magnanimous
when he jumped with a roaring heart
telling tales of outspread skies,
You should have seen him
passionately describe museums aesthetic
for clouds, for adventures
his feet that sprinted till his lungs filled up
like a gypsy he ran
to taste the globe in its tinted glory
with fire bleeding through his lips
and courage etched on his skin
like a maniac he raced
with thirsty wishes outpouring,
You should have him
walk the gentleman's guide to a content life
gifted with some adrenaline

mixed with flirty smiles
ask him to settle
witness his unfathomable wishes fly
one moment looking into my eye
next you know, miles away, this ceaseless guy,
"This can never be me!" He scowled
to stop, to breathe slowly
to wake up in the same bed
walk down the same street
call the same square home every day,
Mustered great courage to walk I,
into his limitless lines,
"Please stay." Under my breath, I pleaded
until I looked into his eyes
recognized a face I'd kill to see next time
with thunder wrapped on his tongue
I watched him frisk with joy
waving a boarding pass
to the next destination in hindsight
knowing my love was too selfless
to ask him to give up on his style
I wiped my tears sheepishly
knowing this sacrifice will slit like a knife,
Set him free
I kissed him goodbye
left a note,
"Follow your heart,

even if it does not lead to me."
whispered,
"I know I am not your home,
but this planet will definitely be.
prepared I am to pay the cost-
even if your happiness means
erasing all mentions of me."

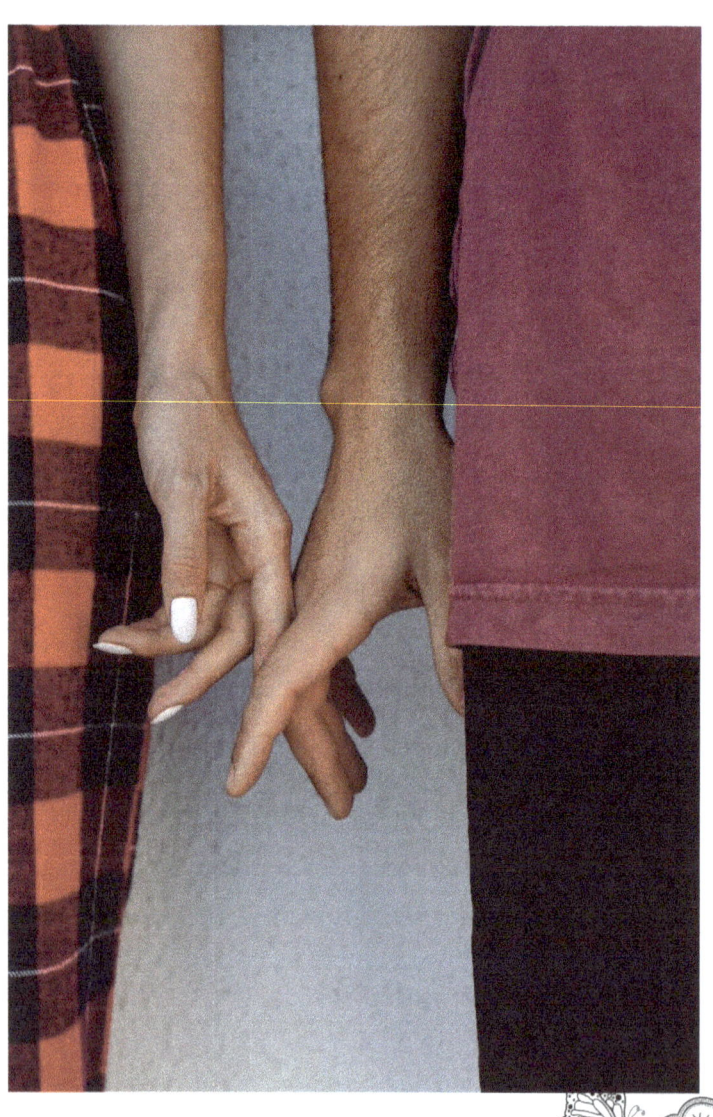

9. ERASING II

Surfing over waves perilous
I left for valleys unnamed
sipped a cup of tribal tea
as I beheld savage volcanoes flaming,
Collecting sand from every coast
I locked it in a jar
and jumped from miles above
until I floated in the air like a cloud,
Assorted stamps and distinct postcards
I wrote to all, near and far
the ticking clock is the alarm of the heart
I reached the port, where aimed my dart,
Ancient temples and hidden treasures
assorted jungles and hallucinatory sculptures
croissant to dumplings to burgers
from Nî Haô to Namaste
footprints everywhere I've left
on every stone I've walked,
Until one fine day,
I lost my path-
looked into the eyes
of a girl,
not knowing how to stop,

Gentle and kind,
the angelic soul silenced my storms
and then she placed her head on my chest
and all I could hear was my heart throb,
louder than excitement any ahead to any spark,
But she was all the differences at war
woods & home & family small
every decision long ago,
I decided to definitely depart from,
I remember her face, when I left for the roads
the utter devastation to hide she fought
allowing me to pull the trigger
knowing the bullet was aimed at her heart,
And now I look at oceans divine
or when I sit weakly in a bookshop
in bits I find myself, looking for her in all,
be it slicing a cake or strolling past lilies
scent of a fragrance or glimpsing at emeralds
and all I see myself do, is find
traces of her in every stranger's laugh,
The only regret I'll ever carry
is asking her to walk away from all these thorns
that she and I are star-crossed,
my abating bucket lists might
choke up her calm simple wish jars,
Began defrosting these walls, I built around
lost in her arms,

terrified of this home I found-
on the passport's call, I ran
for the first time, not knowing the plan
trotting the globe,
filling voids of her loss-
wondering if I could ever admit,
'Afraid I was of what she was doing to me,
hypnotizing me in a way, no journey did'
so I whispered into her ear
"Erasing any mentions of you,
would mean the death of this voyager's heart."

10. ESCAPE

So you know what I did?
I mixed all in the palette
and swirled it in with
some dreamy acrylics,
Sometimes I sewed
day out I sketched,
with tailored scissors
occasionally paper I etched,
When colours drove me insane
I journaled my stories through
pour mud in sluggish pots
bathed my hands in sculpture paste,
When coffee left extra
dipped brushes in them blue,
sponging watercolours
or lazy I-pencil too,
On days I doodled
stuck creamy paste,
with knives I learnt
butter paper is a delicate game,
Alcohol ink I spilt around
a little eyebrow my brushes frowned
some candles I made, few soaps scented,

course then one, on graffiti sprinkling,
My wall a harbour
of perpetual imagination
my slate a reservoir
or creative illustration,
My muse wrapped
In artist works
creative immersive ideas
all in myself I submerge,
You love your lost world, isn't it?
all the time they would say
who will tell them though,
this is my only escape?

11. EYES

Eyes.
Liars.
rest of me, can camouflage
pain and hurt and disappointment, blush
But Eyes.
Don't gawk too deep into them.
they will bleed
I'm afraid what you will see
for the rest of me can laugh
but this black ball
it is beyond manipulation,
Yet so strikingly astounded I am
by how it can fool you
just by what it saw
and rip your brain
out of all other possibilities
deficient of probably, any benefit of doubt,
Like a lone sheep it rests
fixing eyes when a certain someone walks by
or fluttering away when his eyes catch mine
glistening with summer laughter, doomed by winter grays
it is the eyes that begin
that chain of affairs,

Up and down they glance the pristine
providing a chance to feel the world
with stones and jewels, in its naked glory
to feel before any other
organ there is that can proceed,
That is probably why
The Fallen Angel- a painting you cannot deny
telling you tales of ripening sorrow
and eyes only a portal
all whole, for pain to swallow,
Liars.
you can catch a peek of the soul
of every misfortune they've tried to hide
keep staring any longer
only to discover
just the eye
is enough to have you fallen
in love knee-deep with all their crimes.

12. FOR THE LOVE OF IT

Do it
for the love of it,
you don't have to be perfect
neither know everything
do it
for the love of it,
It don't have to be product of capitalism
or one to fetch you money someday
it doesn't have to make too much sense
nor too late to catch up again,
Wake up one day and choose
is it dance, or cook or sew
what is it you wished to learn
before life caught you
up in its hues
and then grip it again
and go for it
for the love of it,
Like an escape like a muse
wander off to childhood
to times when imagination kindled
new rigor in the hands of delight stood,
Do it for the love of it,

forget what they will say
care no more what they will think
this is the world that judges you
based on how you express grief
why care to please people
like this that think?
"For the love of it"
is an explanation enough
and if that doesn't suffice
maybe they're not meant
to understand it after all!

13. FRAGILE

I have tried being perfect
for as long as I can remember
but all I want now
is to be happy,
I have done it all
self depreciative,
stubborn
headstrong
but all I want to be
is gentle on myself now,
I have done many deeds right
favours I shall not name
and if they're still no good
I am fine living crooked,
I have stabbed myself enough
to offer you pieces of me
but if blind is how you wish to be
I will hold the door, for you
in another lifetime, each other we'll see
or maybe not,
I have fought at dawn
with my heart, to wake up and unlearn
many lessons that passers-by

to me have unnecessarily taught
I have broken my bones for you,
tell me,
will you push the wheelchair now?
I have shrunk myself enough
to fit in all that I can encompass
only to realise it's always me
that celebrates others just as they are,
I have been fragile
like a flower for too long
but now I am going to be
fragile like a bomb.

14. HE CAN NEVER

He can never love you
in ways I can-
he whispered into the air
filled with moist in his eyes,
Does he know how you like
filtered coffee with two cubes ice?
does he know what shoe you wear
on a day you wish for luck and health?
He can never know you
in ways I can-
he whispered into the air
filled with bruise on his lips,
Does he know why you don't
talk about love anymore?
does he know why you choose
a lifetime of longing
over seconds of lure?
He can never do for you
what I can-
he whispered to the stars
away far from my glance,
Can you tell him how you feel
at 4 am of dawn?

*can you trust him to bring
treasures hidden in forests dark?
He can never take care of you
in ways I can-
he whispered into the seeping
soil of the ground,
Does he know how to calm you
on a horrendous pathetic day?
does he know which movie
will drive all your pain away?
Probably he will learn
in the lifetimes he has promised to come
stay long enough to unearth
every unturned stone numb,
But there will come a day
he declared glaring into my eyes
you will know what love is
when you will look into his eyes
and wish he did for you
everything in disguise, that I dared to.*

15. I AM NOT A WRITER

In a crowd of pretentious giggles
drowning into loneliness
I am not a writer
I just happen to write,
The way they look at the sky
wipe their hands, I descry
I am not a writer
I just happen to write,
In a conditioned season of understanding
hardly am I understood
I am not a writer
I just happen to write,
Turning bleeding knuckles
into poems euphemistic
I am not a writer
I just happen to write,
In a sea of lovers long buried
embracing every cajolery
I am not a writer
I just happen to write,
Mockery of emotions
mortifying feelings in an alloy of phrases
I am not a writer

I just happen to write,
Broken toy, lost battles
feisty spirit, painless soul
I am not a writer
I just happen to write,
Ink from my brush
morphing into your mirror
I am not a writer
I just happen to write,
Every human yet another
subject of decorative decipher
I am not a writer
I just happen to write.

16. I BELONG

I belong to the mountains
misty and mighty
to grapevines and museums and spring
clinging to European balconies,
I belong to abandoned streets
quiet, viridian, unbothered by misery
to planetariums and aquariums
and glistening bookshops with a tinge of coffee,
I belong to lakes and oceans
and stars that float in lap of the sky
to carved wood and pastel skirts
to some chances I take
forbidden & flattering,
I belong to literature
some phrases I never saw coming
some films, some music
I'm struggling to devour,
I belong to fiction, some facts
some thoughts, ideas, that stayed
to psychology, history and religion
and the very little of me left
in mock tails, macrons, cupcakes,
I belong to the moon, some to the fields

and that lost lover beloved
the face I'll dare never again see
I belong to conversations
chaotic, calm, witty,
I belong to many
but not to platonic attachments
or drunk weekends
or shallow small talk
jealousy, disdain, lethargy,
I belong
but to a legacy of rawness
with not one ounce
of the shadow of futility.

17. I KNOW

I have hoped for better
but worse days have come
I have prayed for remedy
for devastation that never begun
one thing along the way
there is that I've come to learn,
that tomorrow cannot be controlled
neither can yesterday
some moments there are
that dare you to breathe away
some touches there are
that scare you, have gone astray
but one thing I know,
I solemnly know
the anxiety of tomorrow
is not worth trading today's peace
who bickers tomorrow who knows
if today is the last
in this lifetime we greet
too many lists for someday we've kept,
who guarantees misery hasn't already crept?
tired I am that tomorrow you'll walk away
worried I am there's so much left to say

but there's one thing I know
I solemnly know
that tomorrow even if
we're too different to stay
I'd like to believe,
we've at least had today.

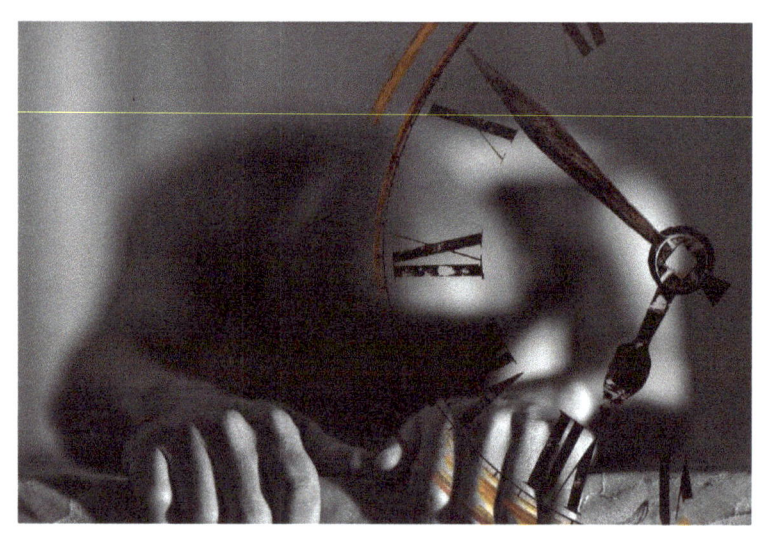

18. IMBALANCE

As much there is to do,
as much there is not
as much there is time
as much there is not,
Time slips from my hands
like grains of sand,
ambitions I have
as heavy as a wet loaded sack,
But when I sit back to recollect them,
blank as paper I stare into the walls
all to realise the gigantic,
number of ticks of the round clock
so far I've lost,
Futile useless in bed all day I lay
and the next thing I know
I'm working next morning
till my sore calves ache,
How is there a balance to strike?
how is there a neutral to hunt?
all I do is burn out
all I do is laze otherwise.

19. LOVED ME LONG BEFORE

He loved me
long before I was smart
or mastered the art of playfully
twirling my hair behind my ear,
Selflessly, unconditionally
long before tragedy
in my heart, burnt a hole
he loved me before
we grabbed a taste of the world,
He loved me
before he prepared me
to bear the wrath of it all
with innocent chuckles and
blossoming flowers
he loved me
till the end of the world,
Long before he left
he walked away having prepared
me to face the world
and although we grew painfully apart
we did so
leaving each other
a little part of our world.

20. MOTHER

I sat by the rusted windowsill,
swiping fingers through the dust in its edge
I give in, this last day
I tried my level best,
Mother
oh mother mine,
silently my head
rests in your lap tonight
no distraught no cure
letterless I abscond
beneath masks of rapture
another tear I hide,
No more to say, no armour to fight
I kneel down on swollen knees tonight
nobody stands by me
I refuse to believe they'd try,
I have offered my all,
yelping, screaming, whining dismay
but now to everyone
'to you your own', I say,
I stay with me when dark clouds visit
when all princes leave me behind
tell me who is stronger

the tortured or the torturer tonight?
Who understands my wars
who understands my loss
nobody gives me a drop
but all for them,
oceans I have brought.
All doors I have locked
all keys I have hung
one last time I latch the door,
Goodbye, mother
see you on the other side.

21. MOTHER, OH MOTHER MINE

Mother
oh mother mine
tonight is the saddest
loneliness of all nights,
Rivers I am drowning
at the bank of my sorrow
hills I am climbing
no ends of tomorrow,
Mother
oh mother mine
I try hard so hard
but lose twice each time,
I am free now
I give up all hope
too much curse
for all stones left unturned,
Mother
oh mother mine
rest my heart in your lap
too much to take, I want to stand back,
A curtain of darkness
a clock of regret
harder in closed fists I tighten

through spaces briskly it escapes,
Mother
oh mother mine
who else do I call
what do I tell them after all this time?
My resting eyes
remind me of dreams that affright
to open my eyes
and reality rots my insides,
Mother
oh mother mine
no matter how hard I try
always aloof a few steps behind,
Mother
oh mother of mine
I trust no enemy
every friend lies.

22. ONCE AGAIN

Once again
you are falling for my words, not me
for my crooked laughter, not me
and my sheepish smile, not me,
Once again
you are falling for our conversations
the scents we exchange
and this adrenaline rush you feel
but not me,
Once again
you are falling for the time we spend together
for the flirty eyes, scissor tongue
for the spice you feel
but not me,
Once again
you will walk away when I pull down my walls
sing songs of melancholy
and tremble as I drop on the kitchen floor
screaming cries of vulnerability,
Once again
I will burn, watching you lose all chords
when I become a habit,
and your appreciation for it all

a long lost cause,
Once again
I reckon
you are falling
for nothing, but the idea of me
you are falling for the tiny sparklers,
not the colossal forest fire
that breathes beneath.

23. OUR CHANCE

We sat by the fence
plucking flowers that stared
"I don't regret it."
he half-smilingly whispered
out of nowhere,
we both have run into
the better suited for us,
leaning back, he
pressed the wooden logs with a sigh,
"I bet." I winked
"This is how it was supposed to be."
happier for, than with
cleverest way, easiest escape,
"But for a second," he stopped
"It felt smooth like sand of a rainy afternoon."
calm and quiet and collected,
"That I wouldn't trade
our laughter,
innocent touch
or popsicles treats
for any riches this world could dish
there isn't a thing I would
change back in times

own tragic terrain drifts."
"It may not have been
the holiest emotion to stand by
that even for a second,
for a heartbeat
for a slip of sand by the fingers,
a glance
you
and I
we were just
like they call it,
eternity's favourite gamble child."
Perplexed I leaned forward,
"Are.. you .. you're saying.. you.."
he smiled with a shiny tear
leaping the corner of his eye,
" I'm not.., anything otherwise,"
he calmly said with fingers over mine,
"We did the right thing," he clarified,
"Any other way.."
confused and blank, I sighed
"We would never know how.."
like a dart he pierced my voice,
That is the point, he chuckled,
"Like adults we ran
at war with our insides
for the bargain we brought

peace to others

an annual interest in alliance."

"But we didn't even trail a shot

tower tumbled before

we even stepped the top

to discern any moment

of finding if

we could have

could have had

the meekest

slimmest

tiniest

of a

chance."

24. PARADOX

Charles Bukowski was happy you think? Oscar Wilde was buoyant?
peace of mind kindled treasures we preserve?
happiness led to greatness?
no my friend, that is a lie,
behind every misfortune is a crime,
behind every masterstroke is a stabbed knife
behind every creation, is a spiel,
Paradox! Paradox! Paradox it is!
that art walks from a place of longing
a masterpiece births from loss
that recklessness relieves the unrequited
that an artist you will find,
not in the neat, articulated, obedient
but in the maniacs, genius, nomads
star-crossed lovers, heartache, whisky and loss,
And not do I wish to glorify pain
but confident I am that these are wounds
that do not bleed but sting the most
muse at the mercy of morphed pain
tacit feelings that failed to cross
of grey matter, the raw loss,
Fuel that burns the vigour to excel,
comes from the realisation

of a misfortune, of a miss,
where agony is the catalyst
wailing, "blood has always been red!"
never poetic, never colourful, never harmonious,
To leave you questioning the mysterious existence of the described,
it leaves you wanting more,
panting with a choked hole,
to allow answers and raise questions
to prick, to please,
art is inspired,
to burn you,
to appease.

25. SHINE

Shine my child, shine
set the devils on fire
shine my child, shine
fear no fear of flying
shine my child, shine
care no more who you blind
shine my child, shine
offend every twisted tongue tied
shine my child, shine
danger shrills as you climb
shine my child, shine
paralyse the need to look behind
shine my child, shine
even when reasons, you fail to find
shine my child, shine
on days the spit, on you is unkind
shine my child, shine
where fear and flight are intertwined
shine my child, shine
especially on days,
you feel dead inside.

26. SPIELS

Bicycles and postcards
reflecting corals all along
carved stones wooden blocks
margarita and piña coladas,
Skateboards and baseball
passports and sunflowers
youth passing
by in an ornate scarf,
Thrill some bets,
romances lasting till diesel's end
pour them in a cup
of relentless resilience,
Lost transcripts
of archaic history
sand and tombs
reduced to ashes of misery,
Marbles carved
into fingers and horns
cream dipped into
veggies sour,
Rave music, shadows neon
throbbing hearts, summersaults
drums and flutes

peculiar to corners abroad,
Wines, some berries
baskets of cane
some spiels of today
will wash away tomorrow's pain.

27. THERE RESIDES THIS HEAVINESS

There resides this heaviness
in my heart beyond my ken
a heavy sack of stones
all stiffened from the pain that loathes
pain from souls that broke me
pain from souls I broke
misery of unfulfilled expectations
misery from long gone stations,
There resides this heaviness
in my heart beyond my ken
an ocean of regrets
a sky of nightmares
all these bushes of grief
that my laughter will
dissolve you to believe,
There resides this heaviness
in my heart beyond my ken
war between a mind
wanting to do so much
and a heart thirsting a pause
begging for a break to touch,
There resides this heaviness
in my heart beyond my ken

a big hole in my chest
burnt to ashes, no mercy to lend
wanting to feel so much
and exactly living in its fret,
There exists this heaviness
in my heart beyond my ken
that on most mornings I seem to have
rigour to push aside, start again
today yet seems like one of those days
that my demons are about to savour my pain,
There exists this heaviness
in my heart beyond my ken
and that only one to understand it
has refused to ever unlock the door again.

28. THE CITY

The city is divine
made of chopsticks and forks
transcending glasses and wooden tombs,
mellows of the sun
set a summer in the sky
with napkins and streets
loyal to the city's fragrance,
chiselled stones, behold one another
to make shapes of agony, some of martyr
the people are hippy
greet you with a glass of beer
sing like the roses,
they dance and their daisies turn to see
all wonders of architecture
all blunders of history
cycles by the bay,
some cherries and pomegranate
all swans and puppies clap
in farmer's markets on Wednesdays
all gather to drown in art
all stroll by to walk by the dark
the city is divine,
made of love and rebirth
they tell you stories
till the stars go off.

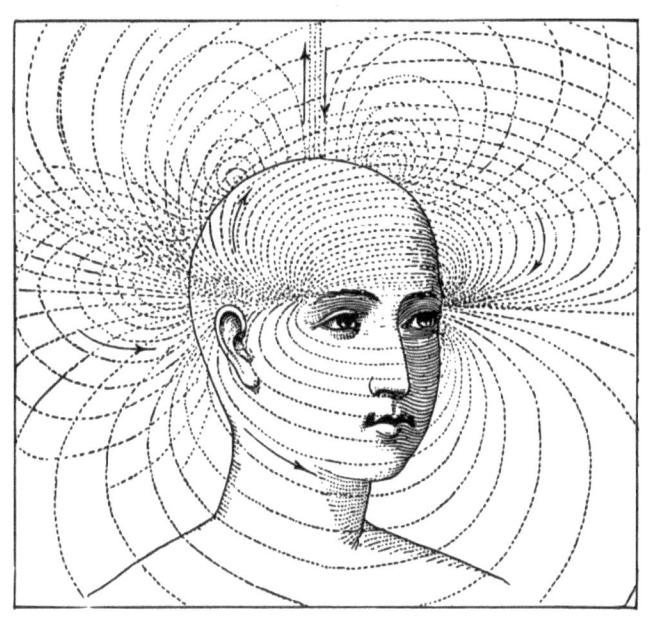

29. THE MIND

The mind is an artist
onerous to define
it lets you believe you are scarred
it lets you hold on to your gains,
The mind is a betrayer
most loyal to thought
it turns into a slave
and switches to a master,
The mind is dynamic
forgets the important
highlights the trivial
fights in fear
and fears in joy,
The mind is brilliant
chemical formulae bond
right body of all shivers
the left side tames and calms,
The mind is stubborn
wants what it wants
until it pulls down its walls
dictates all rules to heart,
The mind is drastic
bends and stretches

like a mother's womb
all set to soak in law,
The mind is underappreciated
the beginning of all revolution
the end of all dust to ash.

30. THE PRICE

They know me for it!
I'd say with pride
getting things done
woman loathing in
"I'll be just about fine!"
Brushing off my knees
wiping the corner of my lip
blinking till my tears reabsorb
sighing as hinges realign,
"Is this the price of virtues?" I'd cry
to be swept by a world
ruined by bird-brained choice
to be patted on the back
for the hits you take,
dumbfounded you're aimed,
I'd cry in my own frail arms
how is it that I choose
integrity and I lose?
pick decisions of stronger skin
left to pick up nothing
but my own broken pieces,
To which my mother
with generosity would reply

"Inner peace is the price my child
no boons, no rewards, no credit points
it is a war a brave
wins silently in the deepest of the night",
You may not sweep in all
but the armed will just walk by
hold you close and press your wounds
long enough till the blood runs dry,
You may not always win,
my mother would claim
"So don't expect fairness", she'd repeat
live your wolfish silence
let the novelty of your nobleness
be remarked by god's own eye.

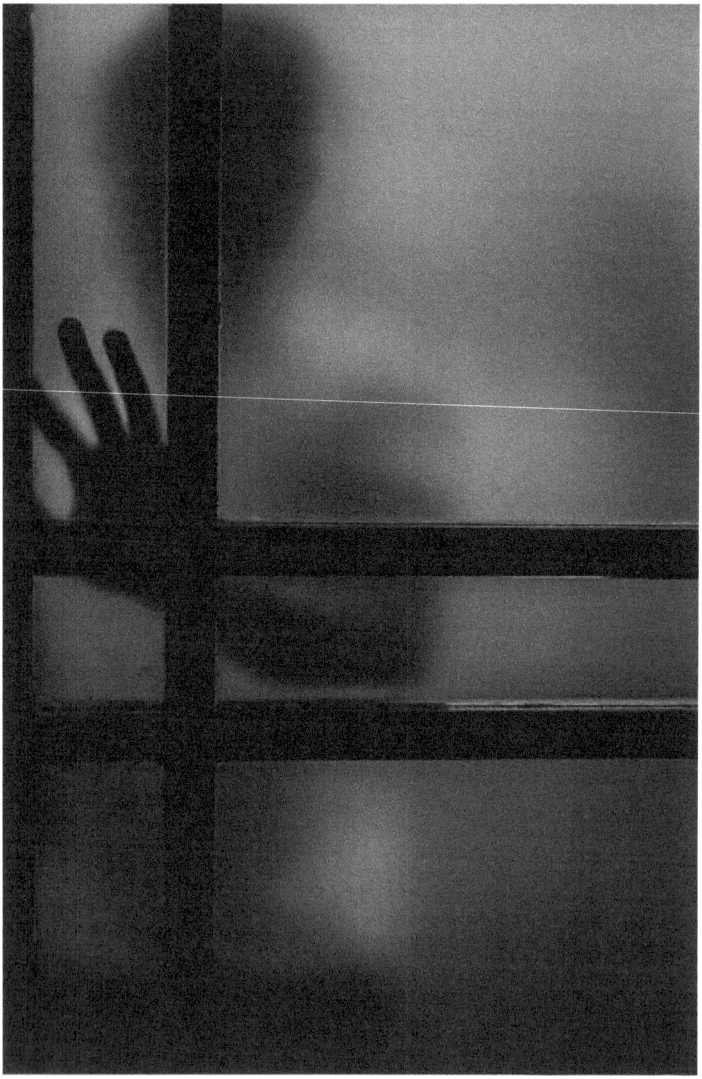

31. THEY ASK ME

They ask me
who it is that I write about
who I hide in metaphors
and beautiful fingers that I'm talking about,
what adventures, whose laughter
what scent it is
in art I hint, with a doubt,
they ask me
if he's real, a fantasy
anyone can exist, with such irony
if truth there is, in all glory
Or just a game of mundane stories,
'What is he like?' describe to me
whose eyes are these, that texture of skin?
what sparkle? what smile?
what lives in him that in others is dying?
is it his speed? is it his voice?
of qualities a plethora, or are my words too kind?
he exists! he does, there is no lie
soft heart, strong mind
of stubborn soul a tie
no less than a masterpiece
a marvel for mankind

so special so sacred
I hide him with my life
he will swirl your world
with ideas and thoughts
and stamp over your heart
of passion a spot
youthful spirit, like aged wine
selfless as much is a swine,
strikingly unusual
to anyone I'll ever meet,
caught up I am
in his thoughts too deep
and if in this life
he is not mine to keep,
'Oh dear universe,
you are the slyest cheat!'

32. THIS IS HER

This is her,
she cries
she howls
she falls
and she crawls
but she welcomes every new morning
with warmth that provokes the sun,
This is her,
she, full of self-doubts
she goes out of the way
she brushes off her knees
and she gets back on her feet
but she greets every single person
as if joy from her, is to learn,
This is her,
she says it's alright
with tears in her eyes
she runs to save you
with all her flesh on fire
but she believes in tomorrow
like she's known never sorrow,
This is her,
she distracts you with laugh soft

nudges and rolling chuckles
only so you don't stare
any deeper into her eyes
but she wears her heart on her sleeve
even if tomorrow it's about to be ripped,
This is her,
too hard on herself
a hungry elf
but a thing stuck once
in her mind and she
never gives up,
this is her,
despite wounds and scars
this is her
she
that always shows up.

33. UNTIL

I have learnt
every single way there is
to lose
until the only option left
was to triumph,
I have broken
in every single corner there is
to shatter
until the only option left
was to heal,
I have cried
every single ocean there is
to weep
until the only option left
was to smile,
I have fallen
every single depth there is
to descend
until the only option left
was to re-emerge,
I have feared
every single thing there is
to happen
and it has happened
and I still stand just fine.

34. WALK

Now that I have learnt,
the blueprint for a perfect lemonade
to fix the bulb & drive quiet
to sit under a starry night
knowing nobody lies beside,
Now that I have taught myself,
to eat solo, celebrate alone
that you won't be here
to smirk at my thoughts,
Now that I have learnt,
to pick myself up
from a hopeless romantic
turn into a realistic beast upfront,
Now that I have walked the shore
so far, sane and alone,
bone to flesh, from dusk to dawn
after all the butchered trust
and pricking thorns,
Now that I have forgiven myself
have remembered to forget you,
like you said you want,
fallen and cried,
brushed myself, & set unchaperoned,

Now that I have lost everything I feared,
and cried till, are left no tears
now that I have victoriously fought
every demon that wore a mask,
Now that I have finally learnt to walk
in all its glory, with faith a path
don't you dare ask for another chance,
or crawl back in,
provoking a murder of the plot.

35. WALLS

My walls of thorns
pitchfork at dawn
they sniff intent
and curl up all along,
Stories they have engraved
of friends turning a fail
of love giving up
resilience with chest impale,
My walls of iron
turn wrists numb
they smile and melt
they frown and harden,
Disdain they have seen
in a failed parent's eye
dreams have shattered
humiliation left shy,
My walls touch the sky
mighty and tall
all who ferociously climb
claim failure to tap the top,
It has seen loud principles
of saints out of window, fly
passing clouds of fever

of lust and power roll by,
My walls spread across forests
no end no tip in sight
go as far as you walk
a mirage of disappointment lies,
It has seen faces change
biting tongues blabbering lies
it has witnessed the world
drag the benevolent
across hell in to a bee's hive,
My heart is moulded
out of an angel,
but Oh my,
love me
for an eternity
or do not touch me at all,
please don't push your guts
against a wall that won't
barge like your other cracked
doors.

36. WAS IT WORTH?

The pain was necessary
it made you who you are
they grin as they pat on my back
but really I wonder if
it was worth the heart I lost?
I was happy
bubbly and hopeful and innocent
now all I look for are flags
red and adherent
a constant battle of emotions
and war of mind and heart,
Tired I am now
while not even half
of youth I've learnt
already doubting sincerest ones
that are nice out of turn,
I wonder if they hate me though
for making them pay prices
of loans someone else took
if putting the kind away
is rattling me more than to them
that it should,
Devastated I am by apologies

that do not even begin
to fix what has burnt
exhausted I am of these walls
for once a parade of blushing roses
are now all lethal thorns,
I never wanted the world
to rust the easiness in me
to trust simply
and I wished to be impressed effortlessly
but all I am doing now
is hunting my own happiness down
before you decide to go too far,
Yes it made me bold
yes they left me cold
but now I wonder if
the wrath that builds inside
is trying to keep me warm
or is about to burn me down?

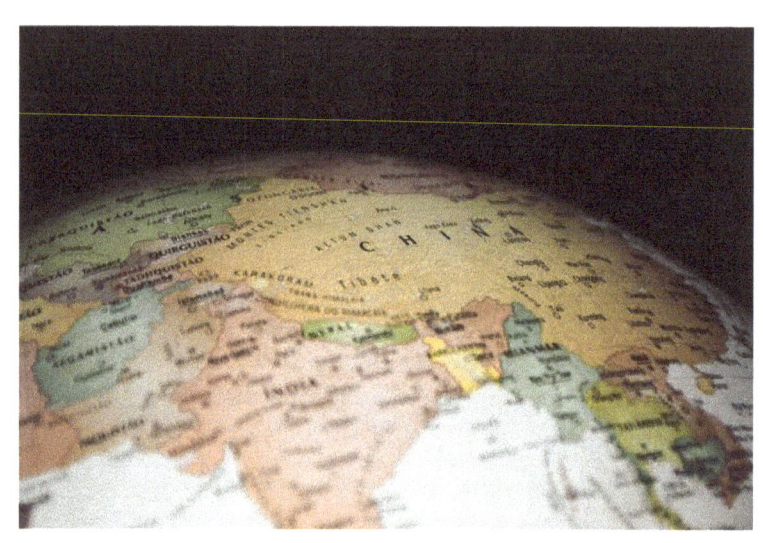

37. WHAT AM I HERE FOR?

What am I here for?
if not to dive into cerulean Polynesia
Or bruise my knees onto Swiss cliffs
sizzlers of Thai and Japanese Shrines
if not to stroll through?
Egyptian pyramids and parks of California
Amsterdam's canals and streets of Argentina
if not to drown a little?
into literature English, Austrian trams
mirroring marbles of Barcelona, Parisian lamps,

What am I doing here?
if not falling a little for Belgian skies
or in the eyes of Berlin, looking for bridges of Budapest
or chanting memories into ears of Czech
what life is this if I haven't?
danced to Italian music, drank cheap wine in Seoul's towers
or thrown ice as confetti in Iceland or foot-tapped over wood in Denmark
what will I have known?
if at the end I haven't sipped Turkish tea
or ran through mud castles of Jordan
or jumped recklessly into Australian clouds

How will I know my heart beats?
if I haven't camped with Russian vagabonds
or watched roaring wilds of Kenya
if I haven't widened eyes in amaze to
violent delights and their violent ends,
What I am afraid of
is a mundane tasteless rat race
that never permits me to fall in love
with festivals and sports and customs
with nations all over the world,
to be dissolved into such ceaseless mediocrity
that you forget there's more to life
than proving to everyone you have one.

38. WHO WILL TEACH ME?

Why did they never teach me
how to love myself above all,
that I pour and pour and pour
each time to land an empty cup,
Why did they never teach me
how to stop loving at once,
theorems and integration
none help when you're out of luck,
Why did they never teach me
that the world will treat you no better
just because you're a good person,
and sometimes that is all
you ultimately deserve to learn,
Why did they never teach me
enduring pain is no talent,
that givers have to draw the line
because takers will never decline,
Why did they never teach me
how to save, where to invest,
terrified I am of tomorrow
because the sea is just
an ocean of all that thrives,
Why did they never teach me

to be happy at all costs
chasing dreams and striking checklists,
who is going to teach me
to pull out the sword
before the storm welcomes.

39. WHY?

I asked God once
why these battles for months?
my tears dry by when,
you prepare another fight;
The road is blur
my faith obscure
I rely on you now
I put all armour down;
A saint I am
no foul I play
which sins are these
whose price I must pay;
All control I let go
no spirit in me is left
in shackles I am
stepping down your list
of silver badge soldiers;
Very silently I wept
after all lights slept
with swollen eyes I asked
"God, what is this ridiculous task?"
Quietly he whispered
in my ear at midnight
I am preparing you just wait,

my beloved
to believe in miracles, my child;
You asked for strength
I sent the waves
you asked for cake
I sent the batter made
you asked for success
the ladder I laid;
Still you are worried
how you will make it that far?
this golden light will shine
to show you god
lives on the other side of war;
Where no luck
no fate, no persistence strives
there god reigns
on disbelief's shrine
when you pass your blurry nights,
on the other side you will find
god qualifying you
for fates which only
for you were destined.

40. YEARS I THINK IT TOOK ME

Years I think it took me
to know some decisions
had no intent to hurt me
taken in favour of one way
but I'm sorry that it broke me,
Years I think it took me
to know all anger
only embraces grief
every act of nonchalance
is yet a route to dwarf agony,
Years I think it took me
to understand you and me
don't have to scoop kindred interest
to be kind a good human,
periodically better than intelligence divine,
Years I think it took me
to appreciate the reasons we all had
none was wrong neither was right
we're all only unfastening claws
to save the little innocence of our lives,
Years I think it took me
to understand the point of doing things
is not be perfect at them

it is only to learn more
about ourselves in the bettering process,
Years I think it took me
to confess I like simple things
raw mornings and folded sheets
that every action little or much
is just a way to feel better in a gigantic rush,
Years I think it took me
to understand what others see in the world
is only what they carry in their heart
that sometimes I clasp too tightly
but I think letting go is the bravest act so far.

41. YOU AND I

*You and I were nothing
but you looked at me and whispered
"around you I am not scared of myself"
I knew we were not nothing,
You and I were nothing
but you'd tell me more about your dreams
of ideas that otherwise you didn't leak
I knew somehow, we were not nothing,
You and I were nothing
but you'd let me stay in your pain
and I'd invite you to my crime
I guess I knew, we were not nothing,
You and I were nothing
but your friends would see us laugh
leaning over to goof up talks
I knew, I knew we were not nothing,
You and I were probably nothing
until one fine day
I could feel you start to slip away
like sand in my hand
the tighter I caught, the farther it flee
and nothing you said
and nothing I did*

our demons fed
on our insecurities
nothing to call it none to blame
I could feel my heart rip inside me chest,
You were right though
when you said we were nothing
but I wonder then why
you took pauses to say it
as if you knew,
we were not nothing.

42. ZILLION OLD

A zillion old
tickets I have left
fair few museums
rest old cafes,
With friends girl-friends
concerts I went
bills that outweighed
coins in pockets,
Some of road maps, other times movies
much of Van Gogh, some airplanes
fleas, stand-ups, seldom lounge talks,
But when I look back
like old days gone by,
ink on these papers
crumpled run dry,
I look at faint alphabets,
find docile laughter
puns that stayed
long after our absence,
A zillion tickets I freeze,
dusty, old, crumpled glee,
remind me of tête-à-tête
submerged deep inside

sniper sure shaped me,
I sit back and meditate,
places or people
what am I holding on?
nostalgia of what was?
or melancholy or what it can never again be?
But then I clasp it tighter
classic call it good-ol-days
memories of what
for a heartbeat
adolescence had been.

www.ingramcontent.com/pod-product-compliance
Lightning Source LLC
LaVergne TN
LVHW061630070526
838199LV00071B/6633